BEST OF
DUBLIN
A GUIDE TO CITY
& COUNTY

JOHN GIBNEY

THE O'BRIEN PRESS
DUBLIN

Dublin viewed from the mouth of the River Liffey, with the Poolbeg Lighthouse in the foreground.

ABOUT THE AUTHOR

John Gibney is a historian with the Royal Irish Academy's Documents on Irish Foreign Policy project. Prior to this he finished a PhD at Trinity College Dublin and worked in heritage tourism in Dublin for over fifteen years. His books include *Dublin: A New Illustrated History* (2017) and *A Short History of Ireland, 1500–2000* (2017).

A Georgian doorway on Merrion Square, with the distinctive fanlight above the door.

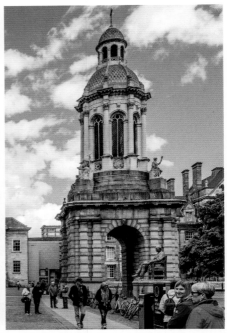

CONTENTS

**Photos on p. 4 (clockwise from top left):
Temple Bar; the Campanile in Trinity College;
Grattan Bridge; deer in the Phoenix Park.**

**Photos on p. 6 (clockwise from top left):
Grand Canal; Fusilier's Arch, St Stephen's
Green; Fairy Castle on Ticknock Hill; Howth
Harbour.**

Overview of Dublin

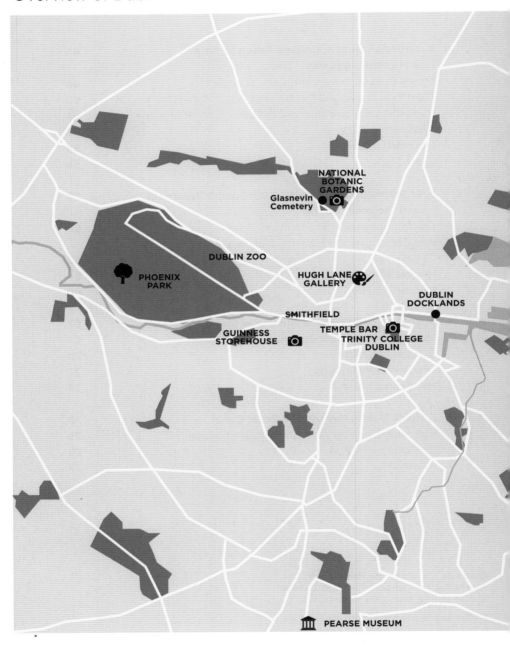

SAINT ANNE'S PARK

BULL ISLAND

HOWTH

NDYMOUNT

DÚN LAOGHAIRE

SANDYCOVE

N

2 km

Central Dublin

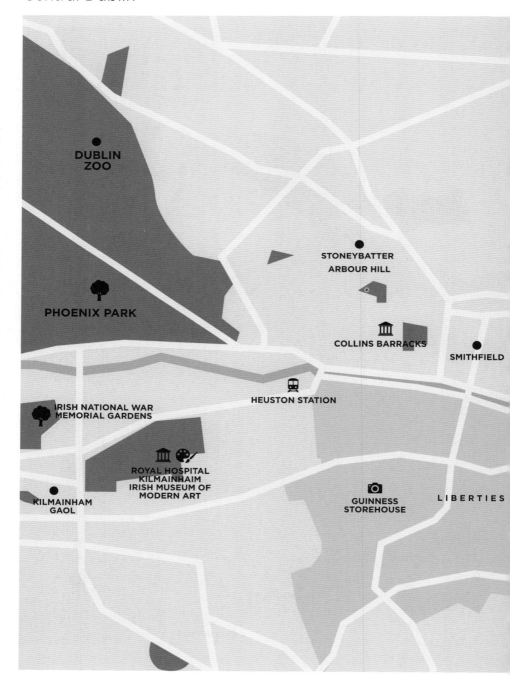

DUBLIN ZOO

PHOENIX PARK

STONEYBATTER
ARBOUR HILL

COLLINS BARRACKS

SMITHFIELD

HEUSTON STATION

IRISH NATIONAL WAR
MEMORIAL GARDENS

ROYAL HOSPITAL
KILMAINHAIM
IRISH MUSEUM OF
MODERN ART

KILMAINHAM
GAOL

GUINNESS
STOREHOUSE

LIBERTIES

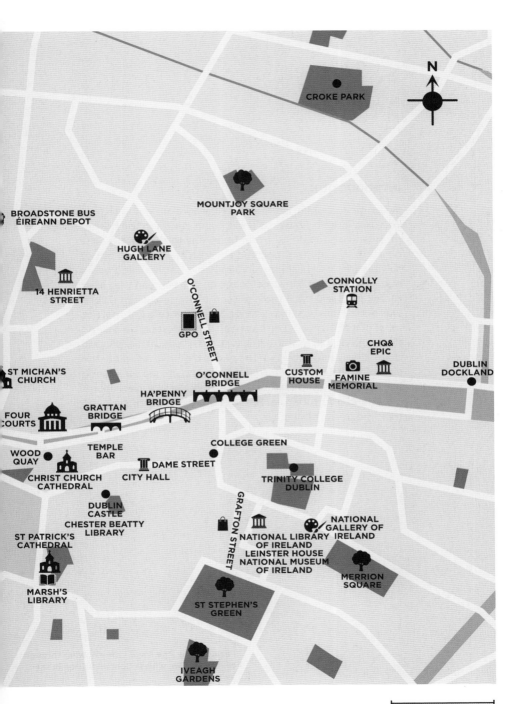

N

CROKE PARK

MOUNTJOY SQUARE
PARK

BROADSTONE BUS
ÉIREANN DEPOT

HUGH LANE
GALLERY

CONNOLLY
STATION

14 HENRIETTA
STREET

O'CONNELL STREET

GPO

ST MICHAN'S
CHURCH

CUSTOM
HOUSE

CHQ&
EPIC

O'CONNELL
BRIDGE

FAMINE
MEMORIAL

DUBLIN
DOCKLAND

HA'PENNY
BRIDGE

FOUR
COURTS

GRATTAN
BRIDGE

WOOD
QUAY

TEMPLE
BAR

COLLEGE GREEN

CHRIST CHURCH
CATHEDRAL

DAME STREET

CITY HALL

TRINITY COLLEGE
DUBLIN

DUBLIN
CASTLE

GRAFTON STREET

ST PATRICK'S
CATHEDRAL

CHESTER BEATTY
LIBRARY

NATIONAL
GALLERY OF
IRELAND

NATIONAL LIBRARY
OF IRELAND
LEINSTER HOUSE
NATIONAL MUSEUM
OF IRELAND

MARSH'S
LIBRARY

MERRION
SQUARE

ST STEPHEN'S
GREEN

IVEAGH
GARDENS

0.5 km

INTRODUCTION

Welcome to Dublin! In this short guide we are going to take you on a journey, in words and images, through the history of Ireland's capital city from its origins to the twenty-first century. The city that became the Irish capital grew out of settlements established by Vikings over a thousand years ago, and much of the streetscape and street plan that exist today are a legacy of the eighteenth-century, when Dublin was one of the most important cities in western Europe. For most of its history, Dublin has been the largest urban area on the island of Ireland, and in the twentieth century it expanded dramatically into suburbia. The pages that follow explore the city through its architecture, buildings and unique sites, along with its history and culture, and expand to include Dublin's hinterland and suburbia. But, as with everything, we need to begin at the beginning.

Facing page: The River Liffey flowing through central Dublin, with O'Connell Bridge in the foreground.

An early twentieth-century Dublin lamp post with a shamrock motif.

1
THE OLD CITY

VIKINGS

Dublin was founded by the Scandinavian raiders known as Vikings, but virtually nothing of their city remains, at least not above ground. The modern city of Dublin evolved from settlements founded by the Vikings from the 840s onwards (though the area in and around what became Dublin was inhabited long before they arrived). Originally raiders attacking the Irish coast, mostly from Denmark, the Vikings soon established more permanent bases around the coast in order to strike farther inland.

The Dublin region was an obvious location: it was on the east coast, at the mouth of a river sheltered in a bay. The Vikings settled at the junction of two rivers, the Liffey and the Poddle, which formed a natural harbour; here, they established their maritime base, or *longphort*. The Irish term for this geographical feature – *Dubh Linn*, a dark or black pool – gave the city its traditional anglicised name, and it was located on or beside the site of the circular garden outside the Chester Beatty, within the grounds of Dublin Castle. It can take a leap of the imagination to visualise the Viking city but Dublin, as it exists today, would not have come into being without it.

The Ballinderry Sword: this ninth-century Viking sword, made in Germany, was discovered in the Irish midlands, having possibly been imported via Dublin © National Museum of Ireland.

WOOD QUAY

Viking Dublin lay on the southern banks of the River Liffey, in and around the modern location of Wood Quay, which houses the main offices of Dublin City Council (the municipal authority). When the council offices' foundations were dug in the 1970s, layers of the modern city were stripped away to reveal the Viking city that lay beneath. What followed was one of the largest excavations of a Viking archaeological site undertaken anywhere; the fact that the excavations were eventually built over was a source of enduring controversy. A fragment of the old city wall can be seen in the middle of the office complex, with the most substantial sections of the medieval city wall surviving on nearby Cook Street.

What can also be seen along the pavements in this area are monuments and replicas of what was found: *Báite*, the sculpture of a Viking longboat by artist Betty Newman Maguire on Essex Quay, the outlines of Viking houses embedded on the pavements at the northwest corner of Christ Church, and the bronze replicas of Viking artefacts scattered along the pavements around Wood Quay. The most eye-catching of these include a piece of Viking graffiti carved onto a plank, and a slave collar. Viking Dublin was eventually part of a trading empire that stretched from Iceland to Asia, and the trade in slaves was part of this. The history of Viking and medieval Dublin can be explored in more detail at Dublinia, the dedicated interactive museum located in the former Synod Hall directly across from Christ Church Cathedral.

▲ dublinia.ie

The 1988 sculpture *Báite*, by Betty Newman Maguire, is made of steel, oak and bronze, and evokes the image of a Viking longboat.

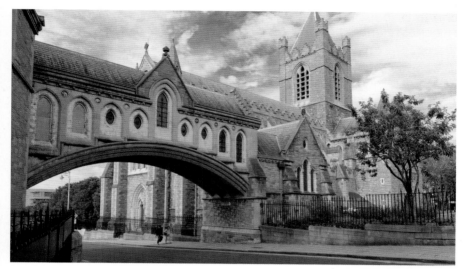

▲ christchurchcathedral.ie

CHRIST CHURCH CATHEDRAL

Prior to the 1600s, Dublin's buildings were mostly made of wood, which is one reason why so little of the original city has survived. An exception, however, is Christ Church Cathedral. Built on a ridge in the 1170s by the English and Welsh adventurers of Norman ancestry who invaded Ireland after 1169, Christ Church lay at the heart of medieval Dublin. It is on the site of an earlier church built by Sitric Silkbeard, a Viking king of Dublin who converted to Christianity. Christ Church has been heavily renovated over the centuries: much of the exterior was rebuilt in the nineteenth century, and the adjoining Synod Hall, which now houses Dublinia (a 'living history' museum) and which is connected to the cathedral building by an archway across Winetavern Street, dates from 1875. But the spire of Christ Church as it stands today can be recognised in a sixteenth-century woodcut, and the interior of

the cathedral retains much its medieval fabric. Like its counterpart, St Patrick's, it is a cathedral of the Church of Ireland, the episcopal church founded during the Reformation, which was Ireland's official state religion until 1869. The crypt explores the history of the cathedral through a wide range of displays and artefacts, including, famously, the mummified bodies of a cat and mouse which got stuck in an organ pipe.

At the eastern end of Christ Church is Fishamble Street, which runs down to the River Liffey and which took its name from the fish market located here during the Middle Ages. It has a small but important role in musical history: on 13 April 1742, the first performance of *Messiah*, written by the German composer George Frideric Handel, received its premiere in a music hall (long gone) on the street. The anniversary is usually marked by a public performance of extracts from *Messiah* on the street.

CITY HALL, DUBLIN CASTLE AND THE CHESTER BEATTY

At the junction of Parliament Street and Dame Street, just east of Christ Church, stands Dublin City Hall, originally opened in 1782 as the Royal Exchange. The beautiful rotunda is usually open to the public, and a close look at the exterior will reveal the marks of small-arms fire: City Hall is a veteran of the Easter Rising of 1916, when it was briefly occupied by insurgents seeking Irish independence from Britain. It was seized because it lay beside Dublin Castle, which housed the British governments that ruled Ireland until 1922.

Dublin Castle is best entered through the gate to the Upper Castle Yard, beside City Hall. At first glance it may not look like a traditional castle. It was built from 1204 onwards, with the River Poddle serving as a natural moat to the south and east. It never had a central keep, though some of the medieval corner towers survive today. The foundations of the older structures can be seen beneath the more modern buildings (but are accessible only by tours). By the seventeenth century, it had fallen into disrepair and much of the existing complex was rebuilt after a fire in 1684. The Upper Castle Yard consists of terraces of offices and administrative buildings, including the ornate state apartments.

Notable buildings in the complex include the elaborate Gothic Chapel Royal in the Lower Castle Yard, completed in 1814, while the castle is also home to the Chester Beatty, which contains the extraordinarily rich collections of artefacts, books and manuscripts acquired by the Irish-American mining

magnate Alfred Chester Beatty, who donated his collections to the Irish state after settling here in 1950. They have been housed here since 2000. In front of the library is the garden located on the approximate site of the original *Dubh Linn*, while behind it, on Ship Street, are the old barrack quarters, which housed British troops until 1922.

▶ **dublincastle.ie**

▶ **chesterbeatty.ie**

From top: The Chester Beatty; A display in the Chester Beatty; An interior view of the rotunda of Dublin City Hall.

Facing page: The Bedford Tower, located in the Upper Castle Yard of Dublin Castle and completed in 1761.

ST PATRICK'S CATHEDRAL

St Patrick's is the national cathedral of the Church of Ireland and is the second of Dublin's two cathedrals. The current building was constructed from the 1220s onwards and, like many other locations in Ireland, was associated with the fifth-century Welsh missionary Patrick, who reputedly baptised converts to Christianity at a nearby well. Like Christ Church, St Patrick's was built on the site of an earlier church but, unlike its counterpart, it was outside the city walls. The spire dominates the skyline in this part of the city. The cathedral tower (known as Minot's Tower, after one of the archbishops) dates from the fourteenth century and the spire itself was added in 1749.

St Patrick's is most famously associated with Jonathan Swift, author of the classic satire *Gulliver's Travels* (1726), who spent most of his career as dean of the cathedral, and who is buried inside. A more obvious but lesser-known association is with the Guinness brewing dynasty. St Patrick's was extensively renovated in the late nineteenth century, and the work was paid for by the Guinness family. They also funded the construction of St Patrick's Park beside the cathedral and the distinctive red-brick Iveagh Trust buildings on the northern side of the park.

▶ stpatrickscathedral.ie

The ornate interior of St Patrick's Cathedral, looking along the choir.

MARSH'S LIBRARY

Beside St Patrick's is the modest but elegant structure of Marsh's Library, named after the archbishop of Dublin, Narcissus Marsh, who oversaw its foundation. Established in 1707, it was opened for the use of 'graduates and gentlemen' and has the distinction of being the first public library in Ireland. While small, its collections are extremely rich and are showcased in rolling exhibitions curated by the library staff. The original collections belonged to Marsh himself and reflected his interests in science and languages.

His collection was added to by the first librarian, the French Huguenot Elié Bouhéreau. Readers over the centuries have included Bram Stoker (author of *Dracula*) and James Joyce (author of *Ulysses*). The interior of the library was modelled on that of Oxford's Bodleian Library, and has one very distinctive security feature: a set of three cages into which readers were locked to peruse the books, which had to be returned before they were let out.

▶ marshlibrary.ie

THE LIBERTIES

The area west of St Patrick's Cathedral is traditionally known as the Liberties. The name itself goes back to the Middle Ages, when distinct jurisdictions – 'Liberties' – outside Dublin's walls were administered by various noblemen and churchmen. Over time, the name was applied to the entire district. Traditionally, the Liberties was associated with artisan trades. It was on the edge of the city with a number of rivers and watercourses running through it. Textiles, brewing and distilling became important industries in the area. Many of these declined in the nineteenth century, undermined by competition from Britain, and poverty became increasingly widespread throughout the area. Many of the distinctive red-brick houses in the Liberties were built towards the end of the 1800s to replace tenements and slums. The Liberties, centred in and around Francis Street and Meath Street, remains one of the most famous districts of Dublin's inner city.

▶ libertiesdublin.ie

HUGUENOTS

The Liberties is often associated with Huguenots: French Protestants who fled religious persecution in their homeland at the end of the seventeenth century. Many were highly skilled, and so were often encouraged to settle in Britain and Ireland. Some certainly settled in the Liberties, working in textiles, but Huguenots were found throughout the city, and there were perhaps 3,600 members of the community in Dublin by 1720 (a dedicated Huguenot cemetery can still be seen on Merrion Row, to the east of St Stephen's Green). Many were prominent in the gold and silver trades as craftsmen. One of the chapels in St Patrick's Cathedral, the Lady Chapel, regularly hosted services in French for Huguenots, and Dublin had a lively French-speaking community for much of the eighteenth century.

The Huguenot Cemetery on Merrion Row, originally opened in 1695.

BREWING AND DISTILLING

The Liberties was very well supplied with water, so it is no surprise that brewing and distilling were prominent here. Traditionally, Dublin had relatively little heavy industry, and some of the city's biggest employers in the modern era were producers of food and drink. Brewing and distilling made the Liberties into one of Dublin's only real industrial quarters. There were dozens of breweries across the city in the eighteenth century but, by the nineteenth century, distilling had become more prominent, and the drinks industry employed thousands in the Liberties.

A notable landmark is the old windmill of the original Roe's distillery on the northern side of James Street, completed in its current form in 1805 and topped with a distinctive tapered copper dome. Many breweries and distilleries in the area went out of business over time – the National College of Art and Design, on Thomas Street, is located in what was once the Powers Distillery. Legally, whiskey can only be called whiskey if it has been matured for three years, and the twenty-first century has seen a resurgence of distilling in the area. There is a dedicated Irish Whiskey Museum on Grafton Street, beside College Green.

▶ irishwhiskeymuseum.ie

Above: The art deco power station of the Guinness Brewery on James Street, built in the 1940s and now home to Roe & Co. distillery.

GUINNESS STOREHOUSE

The Guinness Storehouse is one of the most substantial Victorian industrial buildings in Dublin. Arthur Guinness established a brewery near St James's Gate in 1759. With the growth of rail networks in the nineteenth century, Guinness expanded its market outside Dublin, and left a huge imprint on the city as it grew. It also squeezed out many of its competitors in the Liberties, often incorporating their premises into its own.

The imposing buildings that line the west end of James Street are reminders that Guinness was the largest brewery in Ireland from the 1830s onward and by the end of the century it was the largest in the world. The Storehouse was completed in 1905 and now houses the enormously successful visitor centre. It is located on a distinctive semicircular crescent that was originally a dedicated harbour for the brewery, located on a spur of the Grand Canal that has since been filled in: another sign that the Guinness brewery has been a very large operation for a very long time.

▶ **guinness-storehouse.com**

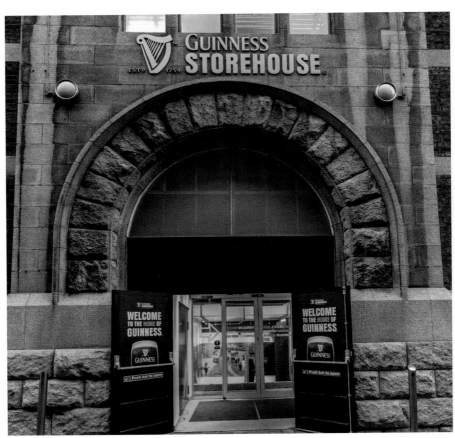

2
The River Liffey from Islandbridge to the Docklands

LIFFEY BRIDGES

Much of Dublin's history has been shaped by the River Liffey, and there are approximately two dozen bridges over the Liffey, most of which are in the city centre itself, east of Heuston Station (the main railway terminus in the west of the city). When the Vikings arrived, the Liffey was much wider than it is today: over the centuries, it has been gradually confined between the stone quay walls. Since the late seventeenth century, it has been crossed by a wide variety of bridges, from traditional stone arched constructions, to cast-iron Victorian structures and more contemporary bridges, such as the James Joyce Bridge (2003) and Samuel Beckett Bridge (2009), both designed by the Spanish architect Santiago Calatrava.

The oldest permanent crossing point, dating from the late seventeenth century, links Capel Street and Parliament Street at the west end of Temple Bar, though the relatively modern Grattan Bridge (1875) replaces earlier structures. The most famous bridges over the Liffey are O'Connell Bridge (1880), which has the distinction of being slightly wider than it is long, and the cast-iron Ha'penny Bridge (1816), also known as the Metal Bridge but which acquired its most common name due to its original use as a toll bridge. It has become an iconic landmark in the city, and one of the most recognisable symbols of Dublin.

Right: Grattan Bridge.

Below: The Ha'penny Bridge.

THE FOUR COURTS

West of Grattan Bridge, the view along the river is dominated by the green dome of the Four Courts. Built at the end of the eighteenth century to a design by Thomas Cooley and James Gandon, it is one of the most notable Georgian buildings in the city. It was built to house the main system of courts, which were clustered in and around here and Christ Church, and it is effectively the headquarters of the Irish judicial system, housing both the high and supreme courts. The dome was intended to compensate for the fact that the imposing facade was not always visible due to the bend in the river.

On close inspection, it is revealed to be battle scarred: the Four Courts was the scene of fighting during the Easter Rising of 1916 and again at the outbreak of the Irish Civil War in 1922, when it was bombarded and severely damaged by the forces of the new Irish Free State; it was reconstructed in the 1920s. The marks of small-arms fire are particularly visible on Church Street, to the west. During the fighting in 1922 a huge explosion destroyed the Record Treasury of the Irish Public Record Office and, in the process, destroyed vast quantities of historical records dating back to the Middle Ages. Copies of many of these have been retrieved from archives worldwide and in June 2022 were made accessible through an online reconstruction of the original building as the pioneering Virtual Record Treasury of Ireland. The more recent office block that can be seen from Church Street stands on the site of the original building.

▶ **virtualtreasury.ie**

SMOCK ALLEY THEATRE

Crossing to the southern side of the Liffey, we come across Smock Alley Theatre, beside Wood Quay. Exchange Street, which curves south to run parallel to the river, follows the line of the medieval wall of Dublin, and this is the site of the second purpose-built theatre in Ireland. Smock Alley Theatre was opened in 1662 as the Theatre Royal, the first theatre outside London to receive the title. It was rebuilt completely in 1735, having collapsed on a number of occasions. In its heyday it was mainly used for London productions on tour and in 1747 most of the interior was torn apart after the manager took issue with a drunken student, which led to a riot. The theatre closed in 1787 and was eventually converted into a Catholic church, which was deconsecrated in 1989. In 2009 the site was excavated: parts of the original foundations were found, along with pottery, broken wine bottles and, appropriately, an unknown actor's wig curler. Since 2012, it has been open as a theatre and venue once again.

▶ smockalley.com

TEMPLE BAR

Continuing east along the river on the southern banks of the Liffey brings us to the district known as Temple Bar. This was originally monastic land but came into the possession of the Temple family, who had settled in Ireland in the 1600s, and from whom the district takes its name (like many streets and districts in Dublin, it is named after property owners). Until the end of the eighteenth century, the Liffey was open to shipping traffic up to this point, and Temple Bar was a combination of commercial area and red-light district.

On close inspection you can see that many of its old buildings were originally warehouses, and eighteenth-century exteriors can still be seen on Eustace Street; the elegant facade of the old Presbyterian meeting house (now the ARK children's centre) dates from the 1720s. As more bridges were built, shipping was forced farther east and the area declined. In the 1970s there were serious proposals to replace the entire district with an enormous new bus station. Instead, it was regenerated in the 1990s as a cultural quarter, and now its pubs and nightlife have become fixtures of Dublin tourism.

LIFFEY CRUISES

One consequence of the bridge building was that, slowly and surely, Dublin turned away from the river as new bridges forced shipping traffic away from the city centre. One of the last companies to use the Liffey for commercial purposes was the Guinness brewery, who used barges to transport kegs of beer downriver to be loaded onto ships for export. The barges had retractable funnels that allowed them to pass under the bridges.

Ferries were another traditional way to get across the river. These were discontinued in the 1980s but have recently been revived. Since 2005, dedicated sightseeing cruises along the Liffey have showcased the perspective from the river itself, revealing much of the commercial and industrial history of the city that was otherwise effectively hidden from view.

▲ **dublindiscovered.ie**

▲ **oldliffeyferry.com**

The River Liffey, looking east along the quays.

CANALS AND RAILWAYS

Viewed from above, Dublin city centre would roughly resemble an oval, framed within its two canals, which date from the eighteenth and early nineteenth centuries. The Royal Canal, to the north of the city, and its southerly counterpart, the Grand Canal, both link the Liffey docks to the River Shannon, which runs through the Irish midlands. Both canals were important transport links in their heyday and have increasingly been reopened for leisure purposes in the twenty-first century. Sections of both canals offer peaceful venues for walks within the city.

While Dublin is not a city defined by a tradition of heavy industry, there is a very obvious legacy of Victorian industry in the form of the various train stations that surround the city centre, which hark back to a time when individual rail companies operated their own termini serving different parts of the country. Some are still in use (such as Connolly and Heuston stations), while some of the old rail lines now carry the LUAS light rail system. The most impressive of all is probably Broadstone Station near Phibsborough: built in the 1840s to resemble a Greek temple, it is now a bus depot rather than a train station. The 3Arena, on the north bank of the Liffey near Dublin Port, was originally a train depot linked to the port.

Top: Broadstone Station.

Bottom: A view along the Grand Canal towards the River Liffey.

CUSTOM HOUSE

Dublin's original Custom House was located on what is now the site of the Clarence Hotel, on the edge of Temple Bar, but as new bridges pushed shipping traffic eastward, a new, larger replacement was built downriver; its location would also, conveniently, give a boost to property prices in the area. It was completed in 1785 to a neoclassical design by the prolific English architect James Gandon and was designed to be seen from all sides. The dome is topped by a statue representing Hope, and the building is adorned with carved heads representing Ireland's rivers. The Liffey is the only female amongst them.

The Custom House has been home to a wide range of official bodies throughout its history. In May 1921, it was gutted by fire during the Irish War of Independence, when it was attacked by the Irish Republican Army (a memorial to the Dublin IRA involved in the attack can be seen outside the north face of the building). The attack left a legacy that is still visible on the exterior. When the building was reconstructed in the 1920s, the dome was repaired with limestone rather than the original Portland stone. As a result, the stonework of the rebuilt section is slightly darker than the rest of the facade.

▶ **heritageireland.ie/visit/places-to-visit/custom-house-visitor-centre/**

FAMINE MEMORIAL

East of the Custom House, on the Liffey quays, is a set of sparse, almost skeletal metal figures. This outdoor sculpture by Rowan Gillespie was unveiled in 1997 as a memorial to the victims of the Great Famine (1845–52), in which approximately one million Irish people died of starvation and disease following catastrophic collapses of the potato crop, which was the staple food for much of the population. A similar number emigrated, especially to Britain and North America. The famine had a profound impact on Dublin, as the city was flooded with people fleeing the ravages of the famine elsewhere in the country, many of whom planned to emigrate on ships leaving Dublin port. The location of the statues is intended to reflect the reality of emigration; a matching memorial by the same sculptor, also unveiled in 1997, is in Toronto, a reminder of the emigrant journey across the Atlantic Ocean in the nineteenth century.

THE CHQ BUILDING

The CHQ Building is located on Custom House Quay (hence the name). A new dock (now filled in) had opened beside the Custom House in 1796 as the port continued to expand eastward. George's Dock opened in 1821, and extra storage space was now required for goods. The CHQ Building was designed by the Scottish engineer John Rennie and completed by Thomas Telford in the 1820s as a tobacco warehouse, and was originally called 'Stack A'. Measuring 154 ft by 476 ft (46 metres x 145 metres), this was the largest indoor space built in Dublin in the nineteenth century, and in 1856 accommodated 4,000 people at a huge public banquet marking the return of

Irish soldiers in the British Army from the Crimean War. It now houses a range of shops and cafes, along with EPIC, an acclaimed, privately developed museum dedicated to the history of emigration from Ireland and the Irish diaspora worldwide.

▶ chq.ie

▶ epicchq.com

DOCKLANDS

Dublin would not exist without the River Liffey. It is, and always has been, a port city. The modern version of Dublin's docklands developed in the nineteenth century. They kept moving farther and farther east as they grew but, by the 1980s, many of the Victorian buildings in the older area of the docklands had fallen into disuse. The construction of the Irish Financial Services Centre (IFSC) from the 1980s onwards sparked a revival of the area that has continued into the twenty-first century. Dublin Port is now located beyond the last bridge on the Liffey, the Thomas Clarke Bridge (also known as the East-Link Toll Bridge). The rows of office buildings found before the bridge, on both sides of the river, testify to the transformation of the district since the turn of the millennium.

▶ **dublindocklands.ie**

3
Smithfield, the Phoenix Park and Kilmainham

ST MICHAN'S, SMITHFIELD AND STONEYBATTER

Across from the Four Courts, on Church Street, is St Michan's (Church of Ireland) Church, the current version of which can be traced back to the 1680s but which is built on the site of an even earlier church. Its vaults famously contain mummified Dubliners of uncertain age. Dublin folklore claims one of them to be a crusader, but given that the earliest recorded interment here was in 1685, it seems unlikely.

To the east is the vast open space of Smithfield, developed in the 1660s as a livestock market, a role that survived long into the twentieth century. From the 1780s onwards, the eastern side of Smithfield was dominated by the Jameson whiskey distillery on Bow Street, which is now a whiskey museum and visitor centre. West of Smithfield is the lively urban village of Stoneybatter which, like the Liberties, is characterised by distinctive late-Victorian houses built to alleviate the problem of Dublin's notorious slums. This entire area was historically known as Oxmantown. The name derives from 'Ostmen', meaning 'men from the east', a term for Dublin's old Scandinavian population. According to tradition, many of them were expelled from Dublin by the Normans and settled in this district, near ancient routeways into Dublin. Indeed,

the name Stoneybatter incorporates an anglicised version of '*bóthar*', the Irish word for a road or path. Many of the street names around Stoneybatter were deliberately chosen to reflect what was assumed to be the Viking heritage of this part of the city.

St Michan's Church on Church Street.

Top: Smithfield Square (or Market).

Bottom: The Jameson Distillery on Bow Street.

HENRIETTA STREET AND THE TENEMENT MUSEUM

As Dublin grew dramatically in the eighteenth century, aristocratic districts emerged. Henrietta Street was at the heart of one of them.

The view from the bottom of Henrietta Street, looking up towards King's Inns and the distinctive arched gate leading to the Registry of Deeds, flanked by the tall Georgian house fronts, is one of the most striking street views in the entire city. Henrietta Street was supposedly named after one of two duchesses, both called Henrietta. Of fifteen houses originally built on the street, thirteen remain. Number 14 was one of the last houses built on the street and dates from the 1740s. Like so many houses used or owned by the aristocracy, it was eventually abandoned by its owners in the 1800s. Later in the nineteenth century, it was occupied by various offices and even by troops from a nearby barracks.

The term 'tenement' in Dublin usually conjures up a particular type of dwelling: the Georgian townhouses of the old Protestant landed and business elites that had decayed to become the Victorian slums. By 1873, number 14 had become the first building on Henrietta Street to be officially classed as a tenement: a slum.

By the turn of the twentieth century, Dublin had a higher proportion of its population living in slums than any other city in what was then the United Kingdom of Great Britain and Ireland. The Tenement Museum now housed in 14 Henrietta Street is a pioneering attempt to explore an aspect of the city's history that was often overshadowed by a concentration on its Georgian heritage. The notorious slums shaped Dublin in other ways: many of the first suburbs constructed outside the traditional limits of the city from the 1930s onwards were built to tackle the problems of slum poverty.

▶ 14henriettastreet.ie

COLLINS BARRACKS AND ARBOUR HILL

Facing the Liffey, Collins Barracks dates back to the first decade of the 1700s, when it was part of a new network of barracks built to house the British military across Ireland. Originally called the Royal Barracks, when it opened it was apparently the largest barracks in Europe. It was built around three 'squares' of buildings that enclosed parade grounds; only two of the squares survive.

The barracks was used by the British Army until 1922, when it was handed over to the newly independent Irish state. It was later renamed after the revolutionary leader Michael Collins. In the 1990s, it was redeveloped to house part of the campus of the National Museum of Ireland. As a museum, Collins Barracks is officially designated for Decorative Arts and History and its permanent exhibits showcase subjects as diverse as the work of the internationally renowned Irish architect and designer Eileen Gray and the military history of Ireland. Since 2012, Collins Barracks has also housed the yacht *Asgard*, in which Erskine Childers smuggled into Ireland many of the weapons later used in the Easter Rising of 1916. When used as a barracks, the complex had a major impact on the surrounding area, and many of the older buildings nearby were linked to it: directly behind it is Arbour Hill Prison, originally founded as a military prison, and the Church of the Sacred Heart, once the chapel for the barracks. There is an old military graveyard beside the church, and in it can be found the burial plot for fourteen of the sixteen men executed by the British Army for their roles in the Easter Rising.

➤ **museum.ie**

This page: Palatine Square, Collins Barracks.

Facing page: (top) Easter Rising memorial, Arbour Hill; (bottom) Church of the Sacred Heart, Arbour Hill.

THE PHOENIX PARK

Farther west lies the Phoenix Park, originally laid out as a royal deer park in the 1670s. Famously, it still contains a herd of deer, and has the distinction of being the largest enclosed park in any European city. The name is derived from the Irish term '*fionn uisce*', loosely meaning clear (literally 'bright') water, although there is a monument of the mythical phoenix on Chesterfield Avenue, the main road through the park, near Áras an Uachtaráin, the Irish presidential residence.

The Phoenix Park is dotted with monuments and structures, the most obvious of which is the Wellington Testimonial, an enormous 67-metre-high obelisk, completed in 1861 and dedicated to Arthur Wellesley, the first Duke of Wellington, who was born in Dublin. The enormous bronze bas-reliefs on three sides of the monument depict battles in which Wellington fought, and themes from his political career; they were apparently cast from cannon captured at the Battle of Waterloo. The Phoenix Park had a long association with the British military and was used as a training ground for soldiers as late as the First World War. The deer tend to congregate around the Fifteen Acres, the vast open space on the southern side of the park, while Dublin Zoo, dating from the 1830s, is also located within its grounds. The park offers a welcome expanse of natural beauty in the middle of a modern city.

▲ phoenixpark.ie

The Wellington Testimonial, Phoenix Park.

IRISH NATIONAL WAR MEMORIAL GARDENS

Directly across the River Liffey from the Phoenix Park, at Islandbridge, are the Irish National War Memorial Gardens, designed by Edwin Lutyens (who also designed the London Cenotaph). The gardens were laid out in the 1920s and 1930s to commemorate Irishmen killed during the First World War. While the figure given in the gardens for those killed is 49,000, this was apparently a miscalculation; the actual number of Irishmen killed in the war was in the region of 35,000, and virtually all of them served in the British armed forces. Before Irish independence, Dublin traditionally had a strong military presence, and service in the British Army was by no means unusual, even for nationalists. This became a touchy subject, however, as the struggle for independence came directly after the First World War, and commemorating Irishmen who had served in the British Army during the war became increasingly controversial. The gardens were due to be officially opened in 1939 but this was postponed indefinitely due to the outbreak of the Second World War, and they were neglected in the decades that followed. In the 1990s, they were renovated and finally officially opened. The gardens, which run directly down to the riverbank, are extensively landscaped in a peaceful location, complete with fountains and sunken gardens as well as memorials such as the Stone of Remembrance, a standardised memorial for the dead of the First World War found across the world in military cemeteries and memorial sites for those killed serving in British and Commonwealth forces.

KILMAINHAM GAOL

Moving south, the imposing edifice of Kilmainham Gaol is best known for housing prisoners after the Easter Rising and in the revolutionary period that followed, but it was originally opened in the 1790s as the Dublin county gaol. The original entrance is adorned with a carving of the mythical hydra, a symbol of unrest and disorder. The vast majority of those who passed through its walls were ordinary criminals, many of whom, in the nineteenth century, would have been transported overseas. It was also a place of execution and remains an undeniably atmospheric monument to darker aspects of Ireland's history. It closed in 1924 but was renovated in the 1960s, and again at the time of the centenary of the Easter Rising in 2016. It has also been a regular location for TV and film directors in need of an authentic prison set, with its cinematic inmates including Michael Caine in *The Italian Job* (1969) and Daniel Day-Lewis in *In the Name of the Father* (1993).

▶ **kilmainhamgaolmuseum.ie**

ROYAL HOSPITAL KILMAINHAM/IMMA

Directly across from the gaol lies the Royal Hospital Kilmainham, built in the 1680s on land formerly owned by religious orders. It was originally a rest home for old and injured soldiers, and it continued to fulfil this role up to the 1920s. It was inspired by Les Invalides in Paris, which performed a similar role, and was deliberately located west of the city, where the air was cleaner.

The arch at the end of the main avenue, across from Kilmainham, originally stood on the south quays of the River Liffey. Just off the avenue itself are two cemeteries: on the northern side is Bully's Acre, reputedly the oldest cemetery in the city, with a small military cemetery on the southern side. With the exception of some churches and the two cathedrals, the Royal Hospital is the oldest surviving public building in Dublin and, in many ways – from its distinctive design to its picturesque location – it is one of the most impressive. The complex was extensively repurposed to house the Irish Museum of Modern Art (IMMA), which opened in 1991. Its collections focus on art in multiple forms from the 1940s onwards and are regularly augmented by an extensive ongoing exhibition programme.

▲ rhk.ie

▲ imma.ie

The inner courtyard of IMMA at the Royal Hospital Kilmainham.

4
Georgian Dublin: College Green to Parnell & Mountjoy Squares

TRINITY COLLEGE DUBLIN AND COLLEGE GREEN

If Dublin had a central plaza, College Green would be it. The wide, roughly triangular expanse of College Green has been a venue for public gatherings for centuries and is a major focal point in Dublin's public transport network. Its also houses two of the greatest examples of Georgian architecture in the city. The east side of College Green is dominated by the enormous West Front of Trinity College Dublin, founded here in 1592 on the site of a former monastery outside the old city walls. The main entrance is flanked by statues of two of its most renowned graduates, the politician and writer Edmund Burke and the playwright Oliver Goldsmith. Trinity is often associated with writers, with Jonathan Swift, Oscar Wilde and Samuel Beckett being among its famous alumni. Another notable graduate, who later returned to Trinity as a professor, was the Nobel Prize-winning physicist Ernest Walton. A more recent figure of international standing associated with Trinity is former Irish president and UN High Commissioner for Human Rights

Mary Robinson, another graduate who later became a professor at Trinity, of law, in her case, and also served as chancellor of the university.

Much of the campus was constructed in the eighteenth century, and just inside the front gate on College Green, Trinity's Parliament Square is home to some of the most beautiful buildings in the city. Particular highlights are the Old Library, completed in the 1730s and home to the seventh-century Book of Kells and an extraordinary range of other books and manuscripts (its vast interior gallery was also the model for the Jedi archive in the *Star Wars* films), and the beautifully detailed exterior and interior of the Museum Building, completed in the 1850s. Trinity is regarded as the leading Irish university, though it is not the largest.

The south side of College Green contains an eye-catching selection of Victorian commercial architecture, but Trinity's largest neighbour is the Bank of Ireland, on the northern side. This neoclassical building was constructed between 1729 and 1731 to house the Irish parliament, which was abolished when Ireland officially became part of the United Kingdom of Great Britain and Ireland in 1801. The Bank of Ireland moved in

Facing page: (top) The interior of the West Front of Trinity College Dublin and (bottom) Parliament (or 'Front') Square.

soon afterwards, and has been there ever since. The interior was apparently redesigned so that it could never be used for political gatherings again, but the old chamber of the House of Lords remains largely intact. The building now also houses a cultural and heritage centre.

When standing outside the bank, look up for a hint of its former role: the British royal crest can still be seen above the colonnades at the front of the building. Both Trinity College and the parliament were associated with the 'ascendancy', the name given to the Protestant ruling class of British origin who dominated

much of Irish life from the seventeenth to the nineteenth centuries.

Between Trinity and the Bank of Ireland is Westmoreland Street, which leads down to the River Liffey, and across to O'Connell Street.

▲ tcd.ie

Facing page: *Sphere within Sphere*, a sculpture in bronze by Arnaldo Pomodoro in Trinity College, with the Museum Building in the background.

This page: The Bank of Ireland on College Green.

Next page: Trinity College's famous Long Room in the Old Library.

O'CONNELL STREET AND THE GENERAL POST OFFICE (GPO)

The enormous boulevard of O'Connell Street began life as an enclosed mall in the 1740s, before eventually being extended to the river. Its modern name comes from the nineteenth-century political leader Daniel O'Connell, who is commemorated by an elaborate statue facing the bridge that also bears his name.

The most famous feature on the street, however, is the neoclassical General Post Office (GPO), completed in 1818. Officially, it was the centre of Dublin: distances to and from the capital were calculated from the GPO. The elegant columns on the front of the GPO are supposed to reflect the Nelson Column, or pillar, which was completed in 1809 in honour of Admiral Horatio Nelson (the hero of the Battle of Trafalgar) and which was destroyed in 1966 on the fiftieth anniversary of the Easter Rising, the event with which the GPO is most famously associated. Like some of the other major buildings in the city, the GPO bears the marks of small-arms fire from the rebellion across its pillars and portico.

The building became the headquarters of the rebellion and was destroyed as a result. It was burned to a shell after the British Army bombarded the commercial district around it, causing devastating fires. It was rebuilt and reopened in 1929 and remains a functioning postal centre to this day. The modern version of the GPO extends along Henry Street, which is the main shopping street on the north side of Dublin. Some of the shops are built into the structure of the post office, which was a way of paying for the reconstruction of the building in the 1920s. The official memorial to the Rising can be found just inside the central window: Oliver Sheppard's bronze statue of the mythical Irish hero Cúchulainn. The statue was first exhibited in 1914, two years before the event it commemorates. However, its symbolism of sacrifice leading to a triumph in the face of overwhelming odds was seen as appropriate to mark the Easter Rising, and it was officially unveiled as the memorial in 1935.

▶ anpost.com/Witness-history

The GPO on O'Connell Street.

PARNELL SQUARE AND DUBLIN CITY GALLERY THE HUGH LANE

Parnell Square, at the northern end of O'Connell Street, is the earliest of Dublin's Georgian squares, and was laid out between 1751 and 1785. Originally called Rutland Square, it was renamed in 1933 after the nationalist leader Charles Stewart Parnell, who is the subject of another monument at the end of O'Connell Street. Originally, at its centre was a pleasure garden now occupied by the Rotunda Hospital and the Garden of Remembrance (commemorating those who died in the struggle for independence). The three sides incorporate different styles of house, but the largest and most significant was the limestone edifice of Charlemont House, built in the 1760s for James Caulfield, Earl of Charlemont. It deliberately dominates the northern, elevated, side of the square and was remodelled as the Municipal Gallery (now Dublin City Gallery the Hugh Lane) in the 1930s.

Francis Bacon's reconstructed studio at the Hugh Lane.

Prior to the First World War, the art collector Hugh Lane offered his collection of paintings (including works by modernist and impressionist painters like Manet, Monet and Morisot) to the city for free as long as Dublin's authorities provided a suitable home for them. It was opposed at the time on financial grounds, which prompted W.B. Yeats' famous poem 'September 1913', with its caustic refrain 'romantic Ireland's dead and gone'. Lane himself was killed in 1915 when the liner he was travelling on, RMS *Lusitania*, was torpedoed off the southern coast of Ireland by a German submarine during the First World War. An arrangement was reached to split the collection between Dublin and London, and it forms the core of the gallery's distinctive collections of nineteenth- and twentieth-century art. A notable feature is a reconstruction of the studio of Francis Bacon, who was born in Dublin. The gallery hosts an extensive range of exhibitions, workshops and events throughout the year.

▲ hughlane.ie

ARCHITECTURAL STYLES

Relatively little of Dublin's early architecture survives, and it can be difficult to learn about Dublin's history before 1300, as cellars built in later centuries destroyed a great deal of archaeological detail. Dublin is often assumed to be a Georgian city, but its built heritage owes much to the Victorian era as well. 'Georgian' is the term used to describe the period from the accession of George I as king of Britain and Ireland in 1714 to the death of his eventual successor, George IV, in 1830.

During this time, much of Dublin's existing streetscape was rebuilt, often in a distinct neoclassical style. 'Victorian' describes the period covered by the lengthy reign of Queen Victoria from 1837 to 1901; some impressive legacies in the streetscape that date from this era include the City Markets, including the George's Street Arcade, on South Great George's Street, and some of the enormous Guinness buildings on James Street, which comprise the largest cluster of industrial structures in the city.

Moving into the twentieth century, Dublin also acquired various buildings in other styles: the Government Offices at 23 Kildare Street, completed in 1942, are a fine example of art deco, while Áras Mhic Dhiarmada – or Busáras, the central bus station, which was completed in 1953 – is perhaps the best-known modernist building in the city.

The best way to appreciate Dublin's architectural heritage is simple: look around and look up.

The facade of the City Markets on South Great George's Street.

MOUNTJOY SQUARE

East of Parnell Square lies Mountjoy Square, which was developed by the wealthy Gardiner family from the 1780s, possibly in response to the development of Merrion Square south of the Liffey. It was the last of Dublin's Georgian Squares and is the only one to form a perfect square: the gardens measure 140 metres (450 ft) on each side. It was built on elevated ground and the terraces were designed to emphasise a sense of enclosed space, though the southern view towards the Custom House is an elegant exception. The terraces were built in a relatively modest but co-ordinated style, and the distinctive doors were meant to be the major decorative features.

By the 1840s, Mountjoy Square was a popular residence with the legal profession, but by the 1920s it largely consisted of tenements, one of which was lived in by the playwright Sean O'Casey; it may have inspired the setting for his 1923 play *The Shadow of a Gunman*. Some of the facades on the south and west are replicas of the originals, having been demolished and rebuilt in the late twentieth century. The destruction of Georgian buildings on this scale was one of the catalysts for the campaigns to preserve the architectural heritage of Georgian Dublin that became prominent from the 1960s onwards.

➤ **mountjoysq.com**

CROKE PARK

Towering over the city to the east of Mountjoy Square is one of the largest stadiums in Europe, built for the use of games played primarily in Ireland. The Gaelic Athletic Association (GAA) was founded in the 1880s to promote distinctively Irish sports such as handball, hurling (a sport of great antiquity) and Gaelic football, and the 82,000-seat Croke Park is its headquarters. The site was originally a racecourse but from the 1890s, it was being used by the fledgling GAA and other sporting bodies. It was purchased for the use of the GAA in 1908 and named Croke Park in 1913, after the Catholic bishop who was one of the early patrons of the association. In 1920, fourteen spectators and players were killed when British forces fired into the ground as a reprisal for IRA attacks on 'Bloody Sunday', 21 November.

The stadium also houses the official GAA museum. It was redeveloped into its current form from the 1990s onwards. There is a nearby link to another sporting institution: in the 1930s, FC Barcelona was managed by the Dubliner Patrick O'Connell, who was born a few hundred metres from the current main entrance to the stadium. Croke Park has hosted concerts and various sporting events over time, but it is best known as the venue for what are probably the most prominent events in the Irish sporting calendar: the All-Ireland football and hurling finals, traditionally played in September but more recently in July. Croke Park's inner-city location guarantees that the match-day atmosphere extends to the area around the stadium.

▲ **crokepark.ie**

An All-Ireland Senior Football Final between Dublin (in blue) and Kerry at Croke Park.

5
St Stephen's Green to Merrion Square: Georgian and Victorian Dublin

GRAFTON STREET AND ST STEPHEN'S GREEN

Grafton Street is the principal shopping street south of the Liffey and connects College Green to St Stephen's Green, at its southern end. Here, the park can be entered through the distinctive memorial arch at its most northerly corner. The official name for this is Fusiliers' Arch, commemorating soldiers from Dublin who were killed while serving with the British Army in Africa during the Boer War of 1899–1902. A close look at the side of the arch reveals the marks of small-arms fire from the Easter Rising, when there was fighting in this area. Republican insurgents initially dug trenches in the park in an effort to control some of the southern approaches to the inner city, but they were driven out by British troops and took refuge in the Royal College of Surgeons on the west side of the green, another building with a bullet-scarred facade.

The park that lies behind the arch was first laid out in the 1660s, and a visitor to Dublin at that time would have noted that it stood on what was then the edge of the city. St Stephen's Green is easily the most famous, and popular, of Dublin's public parks, and throughout the eighteenth century it was a site for fashionable promenading and performances.

St Stephen's Green was renovated in the 1870s at the behest of the Guinness family – one of the many sculptures dotted throughout the park is a statue to Sir Arthur Edward Guinness, on the western edge of the park – and the landscaping of the green, centred around its ponds and fountains, dates from that time. Its central location ensures a steady flow of pedestrian traffic through it, but the enduring popularity of St Stephen's Green with locals and visitors can be seen throughout the year.

The privately operated Little Museum of Dublin, located across from the northern side of the green, serves as a dedicated museum to the Irish capital.

▶ graftonstreet.ie

▶ ststephensgreenpark.ie

▶ littlemuseum.ie

Facing page: Fusilier's Arch, St Stephen's Green, facing Grafton Street.

Next page: St Stephen's Green.

LEINSTER HOUSE, THE NATIONAL MUSEUM AND THE NATIONAL LIBRARY OF IRELAND

Leinster House began life as the town-house of James Fitzgerald, 20th Earl of Kildare and later Duke of Leinster, and it was completed in 1745. It was built in what was then a relatively unfashionable area, though the earl supposedly quipped that wherever he built his home, fashion would follow. The combined sense of animation and enclosure that usually surrounds it today arises from its role as the seat of the Irish parliament, Dáil Éireann, which has sat here since the 1920s. As a result, public access can be limited. Leinster House is flanked by two buildings with matching facades, one on either side: the National Library of Ireland to the north, and the original site of the National Museum of Ireland to the south.

These were built in the 1880s. Despite their similarities, the museum is the larger of the two and houses the archaeological collections of the museum, some of which were originally in the possession of the Royal Irish Academy, on nearby Dawson Street. The collections held in Kildare Street include some of the National Museum's most famous artefacts, including one of the most significant collections of Bronze Age jewellery in Europe. Highlights include the elaborate Ardagh Chalice, the Tara Brooch, the Derrynaflan and Broighter hoards, and the Cross of Cong. Alongside these are a wide range of artefacts from the Stone, Bronze and Iron Ages, Viking and Medieval artefacts and, strikingly, a collection of human remains, often sacrifices, preserved in Irish bogs for thousands of years. The books and manuscripts that comprise the treasures of the library are of a different order, but the enormous domed reading room, with its Victorian tables and distinctive green glass reading lamps, is perhaps one of the most impressive interior spaces to be found in Ireland, let alone in Dublin.

▶ **museum.ie/en-IE/Museums/Archaeology**

Facing page: Leinster House.

This page, from top: The eighth-century Ardagh Chalice is one of the treasures in the National Museum; The facade of the National Museum of Ireland – Archaeology on Kildare Street; Reading Room of the National Library of Ireland.

Dublin has had an important part to play in the Irish literary tradition. Many eminent writers have come from Dublin, and Dublin has played a role in many of their works. The most famous is undoubtedly James Joyce, the author of classics such as *Dubliners* (1914) and, most famously, *Ulysses* (1922), which follows a number of characters through Dublin in the course of a single day, 16 June 1904, a date now celebrated annually as Bloomsday, named after the central character, the Jewish Dubliner Leopold Bloom. But there are plenty of prominent writers who were active long before Joyce, such as Jonathan Swift, the author of *Gulliver's Travels;* Bram Stoker, the author of *Dracula* (1897); and Oscar Wilde (who is remembered by a statue in Merrion Square, near his family home). Dublin was the birthplace of three winners of the Nobel Prize for literature: W.B. Yeats, George Bernard Shaw and Samuel Beckett.

At the start of the twentieth century, Dublin was central to the Irish literary revival, as figures like Lady Augusta Gregory, W.B. Yeats and J.M. Synge attempted to create a new and distinctively Irish literature in the English language. The venue for many of their works was the famous Abbey Theatre, located on Abbey Street in Dublin city centre and now the official national theatre.

Even writers more usually associated with rural Ireland, such as John McGahern and Edna O'Brien, have often used Dublin as a setting. Perhaps the most famous writers from outside Dublin to carve out a niche in the capital were the generation of writers active after the Second World War: the American J.P. Donleavy, who studied at Trinity College thanks to the GI bill and who fictionalised his experience in *The Ginger Man* (1955); the Tyrone-born satirist Brian O'Nolan, better known both as the novelist Flann O'Brien and the columnist Myles na Gopaleen; and the Monaghan poet Patrick Kavanagh. Among their contemporaries was the Dubliner Brendan Behan, author of *Borstal Boy* (1958). More recently, writers such as Roddy Doyle have given voice to newer aspects of Dublin's history, setting works such as the Booker Prize winner *Paddy Clarke Ha Ha Ha* (1993) in the suburbs that have sprung up around the city since the 1930s.

The prominence given to writers should not obscure the fact that Dublin has also produced a number of distinctive visual artists, such as Walter Osborne, Mainie Jellett, Evie Hone, Harry Clarke and Harry Kernoff. Many of their works can be seen in Dublin City Gallery the Hugh Lane and the National Gallery of Ireland.

Sculpture of Oscar Wilde in Merrion Square, near his birthplace on Westland Row.

MERRION SQUARE

The rear of Leinster House faces onto Merrion Square, probably the best known and most impressive of Dublin's Georgian squares. At its centre is the other major park in the south of the inner city, which easily rivals St Stephen's Green for popularity. However, being slightly away from the main thoroughfares, it doesn't get the same footfall. The square was laid out from the 1760s onwards and, when Georgian architecture in Dublin is discussed, this square is probably what comes to mind: the Georgian and Victorian terraces that surround it remain surprisingly intact and give a strong sense of the era from which they date.

At the western end of the square are the National Gallery of Ireland and another campus of the National Museum of Ireland – Natural History, usually nicknamed the 'Dead Zoo'. At the southernmost corner of the square, the view along Mount Street Upper leads to the distinctive dome of St Stephen's Church, dating from the 1820s and nicknamed, for obvious reasons, the Pepper Canister. The park contains a diverse range of monuments and sculptures, and, having been recently renovated, it hosts a wide range of events throughout the year. At weekends, the railings around it become home to an open-air art market.

6
South Dublin beyond the Grand Canal

SANDYMOUNT AND SANDYCOVE

The affluent Victorian suburb of Sandymount lies on the south edge of the city, facing Dublin Bay. In the eighteenth century, this contained some of the brickfields from which Georgian Dublin was constructed, but it came into its own as a coastal suburb in the Victorian era, with the distinctive triangular green at the heart of its village.

Sandymount lies alongside the wide, flat expanse of Sandymount Strand. The strand features in James Joyce's *Ulysses*, the opening scene of which is set in the Martello tower at Sandycove. These towers were built as fortifications during the Napoleonic Wars, and can be found around the Irish coast and occasionally inland. There are a number of them scattered along the southern edge of Dublin Bay itself, and another at Sutton on the north side of the bay. The Martello tower at Sandycove, which was the starting point for the first Bloomsday celebration, in 1954, now houses a museum dedicated to Joyce.

▶ joycetower.ie

Below: The James Joyce Tower and Museum at Sandycove.

Next page: Sandymount Strand, with Blackrock and Dún Laoghaire visible in the distance.

DÚN LAOGHAIRE

The rail line that carries the suburban DART (Dublin Area Rapid Transit) network through Sandymount dates from the 1830s, when it was the first railway line opened in Ireland. It was built to link the newly constructed port of Kingstown to the city centre. The original name of Dun Leary was changed to Kingstown in 1821 in honour of a visit by King George IV, but was changed back to the Irish version, Dún Laoghaire, in 1920, as a protest against British rule during the struggle for independence ('*dún*' is an Irish term for a fortified dwelling place, and crops up in many place names across Ireland).

Until 2015, Dún Laoghaire was one of the principal ferry ports on the Irish Sea crossing, and its maritime legacy infuses the seafront and the town. The town is still home to four yacht clubs, with races in the bay being a regular feature. For those interested in maritime history, Dún Laoghaire houses the National Maritime Museum, but the most appealing features of the town for locals and visitors alike are the immensely long granite piers stretching into Dublin Bay, a favourite of walkers. The town itself and its hinterland offer an extensive and diverse range of

Victorian buildings, interspersed with some striking modern structures such vast new dlr Lexicon library overlooking the harbour, which is meant to resemble a sail, and the headquarters of the Commissioners of Irish Lights beside the harbour. They have responsibility for lighthouses around the island of Ireland and so, appropriately, the building is intended to resemble a beacon.

▶ **mariner.ie**

Top: The distinctive outline of the dlr Lexicon library in Dún Laoghaire, with the National Yacht Club in the foreground.

Bottom: The East Pier, Dún Laoghaire.

THE DUBLIN MOUNTAINS

Rising up behind the southern edges of the capital city are the Dublin and Wicklow mountains; and if you look along some of the older boulevards laid out in the eighteenth century (like Fitzwilliam Place or Dorset Street), it is very obvious that the planners of an earlier era realised how picturesque they could be: these roads were laid out deliberately to lead to a view of the mountains. What you can see from the city is the northern edge of Ireland's largest upland area, a huge granite bulge in the landscape, coated with forests and peat bogs.

The border between the counties of Dublin and Wicklow to the south runs through the mountains, so some of them actually are in Dublin. The highest peak, Lugnaquilla, on the eastern edge of the mountains, rises to 925 metres, but despite their modest height, the uplands of Dublin and Wicklow have a bleak beauty of their own. The northern fringes are accessible from the city, with areas like Ticknock Forest and the Featherbeds being highlights within easy reach, while Montpelier Hill and Three Rock Mountain offer spectacular views over the city. This area of the mountains is well served by walking routes and trails, from the Wicklow Way (which begins in Marlay Park) to the more recent Dublin Mountains Way.

Top: Fairy Castle on Ticknock Hill.

Bottom: The 'Hellfire Club', an eighteenth-century hunting lodge on top of Montpelier Hill, in the Dublin Mountains.

Next page: A view over the Dublin Mountains.

THE PEARSE MUSEUM

The Pearse Museum is situated in picturesque parkland in the south Dublin suburb of Rathfarnham and is housed in an elegant late-eighteenth-century house, originally called The Hermitage. From 1908 it housed St Enda's College – Scoil Éanna – the school opened and administered by the cultural nationalist and revolutionary Patrick Pearse, after whom the museum is named, and who was executed by the British as one of the leaders of the Easter Rising.

A pioneering educationalist, Pearse modelled his school on continental styles of bilingual teaching, as well as similar forms of cultural activism in Scotland and Wales. St Enda's was a boarding school, which adopted a child-centred model with a great emphasis on the Irish language, and cultural, physical and artistic activities beyond the classroom, such as plays and pageantry. Many of its students fought in the Easter Rising and the subsequent struggle for independence.

▶ **pearsemuseum.ie**

7
North Dublin beyond the Royal Canal

GLASNEVIN CEMETERY AND THE BOTANIC GARDENS

Just north of the city centre is Ireland's largest cemetery, Glasnevin (originally Prospect) Cemetery, opened in 1832. A non-denominational burial ground for those 'of all religion and none', it is the final resting place for over a million people. It is best known for the Republican Plot, the dedicated space for Irish nationalists and republicans beside the round tower that marks the crypt of Daniel O'Connell, the nineteenth-century political leader who founded the cemetery.

Glasnevin was laid out as a garden cemetery, in which the natural beauty of the surroundings could prompt reflection. Parts of it are heavily wooded and some sections almost serve as an open-air sculpture gallery, with a diverse range of monuments marking the final resting places of an equally diverse range of people.

The cemetery adjoins the National Botanic Gardens, which date back to 1795. Between them, the gardens and the cemetery make up one of the largest open spaces in the city.

The elaborate Victorian glasshouses of the Botanic Gardens frame the skyline to the north of the cemetery, and the gardens contain a wide range of plant species from across the world, as well as a library and visitor centre.

▶ **dctrust.ie**

▶ **botanicgardens.ie**

Glasnevin Cemetery.

The Great Palm House at the National Botanic Gardens.

BULL ISLAND AND ST ANNE'S PARK

Travelling north of the city along the coastal suburbs of Clontarf and Dollymount brings a visitor to Bull Island, the major beach and bathing spot within Dublin Bay itself, and a nature reserve of international importance for migrating birds; it is a key part of the Dublin Bay Biosphere, as recognised by UNESCO. Dollymount is a relatively recent addition to Dublin Bay, as it was formed only in the nineteenth century.

Dublin Bay was notorious for its deceptively shallow waters. To keep the shipping channel clear, the north and south Bull Walls were built. As a result, the tides deposited silt and sand outside the walls, expanding Sandymount Strand to the south of the bay and creating Bull Island to the north. The sweeping expanse of the beach is perhaps as close as you can get to the wildness of the bay while remaining on land.

Directly behind Bull Island, on the shore, is St Anne's Park, which probably has the most picturesque location of Dublin's major parks. It was originally owned by the Guinness family, and its woodlands are dotted with various gazebos and include ponds, a rose garden, a walled garden, an arboretum and a range of recreational facilities. The mansion that stood at the heart of the grounds was demolished after being destroyed in a fire, though the foundations can still be seen at the end of the long avenue that runs from Vernon Avenue to the eastern side of the park.

Facing page: (top) Bull Island, looking towards Howth; (bottom) The Clock Tower in St Anne's Park, Clontarf.

HOWTH

The northern edge of Dublin Bay is framed by the peninsula of Howth, which is connected to the mainland by a narrow strip of land carrying a road and the DART line, which terminates in the village of Howth itself. Prior to the construction of Kingstown (now Dún Laoghaire), this was a major crossing point on the Irish Sea (marked, on the West Pier, by a set of carved footprints commemorating the arrival of King George IV in 1821).

Facing onto the Irish Sea, it is still a working fishing village and a popular venue for day trips. Howth peninsula has been settled for thousands of years. Howth Castle, just outside the village, was until recently the home of the St Lawrence family, who settled here in the Middle Ages, and the ruins of a fourteenth-century abbey can be seen in the village itself. The distinctive Baily Lighthouse, which guards the northern approach to Dublin Bay, is built on the site of an ancient promontory fort.

The edges of the peninsula are ruggedly beautiful and can best be seen via the cliff walk that runs around the peninsula between Howth and Sutton, one of a number of trails on the peninsula. Many visitors begin the cliff walk in Howth, but as the village now has a very large collection of pubs and seafood restaurants, the walk is perhaps best started in Sutton to make the most of a day out.

Facing page: (top) Howth Harbour looking out to Ireland's Eye; (bottom) The Baily Lighthouse.

First published 2023 by
The O'Brien Press Ltd,
12 Terenure Road East, Rathgar,
Dublin 6, D06 HD27, Ireland.

Tel: +353 1 4923333; Fax: +353 1 4922777
E-mail: books@obrien.ie
Website: obrien.ie
The O'Brien Press is a member of Publishing Ireland.

ISBN: 978-1-78849-164-8

8 7 6 5 4 3 2 1
27 26 25 24 23

Typesetting, layout, design © Tanya M. Ross www.ElementInc.ie 2023
Cover design © Tanya Ross www.ElementInc.ie 2023
Editing © The O'Brien Press 2023

Photographs © Shutterstock except for:
P. 3 (Louise Kennedy doorway) © Naoise Culhane; p. 15 © National
Museum of Ireland; p. 16 © Betty Newman Maguire; p. 19 (top and
middle) © Chester Beatty; pp 21, 22 and 51 © Sean Kennedy; p. 56 ©
Piaras Ó Mídheach/Sportsfile; p. 63 © Alamy.
Cover photograph of the Ha'penny Bridge at night © iStockphoto.com.

Cover photographs
Front: (main) Ha'penny Bridge; (bottom, l–r): Grand Canal, Ardagh
Chalice, Baily Lighthouse.
Back: (main) Wellington Testimonial, Phoenix Park; (bottom, l–r): Trinity
College, Howth Harbour, Guinness Storehouse.

Printedby EDELVIVES, Spain.
The paper in this book is produced using pulp from managed forests.

Published in